You Got This, Girl

52 Weeks of Awesomeness

This book Belongs To

....

Great things

NEVER came

from

Comfort zones

Getting Things Done For The Week Of: _____

things to do

Habit Tracker

HABIT	S	M	T	W	T	F	S	REWARD

Water
(Check The Circle For 8 Glass Daily)

Girl you Got This!

SUN	MON	TUES	WED	THUR	FRI	SAT

3 Things I am Thankful For »

7 Goals For Next Week »»»»

Notes »

Getting Things Done For The Week of: _____

things to do

Habit Tracker

HABIT	S	M	T	W	T	F	S	REWARD

Water
(Check The Circle For 8 Glass Daily)

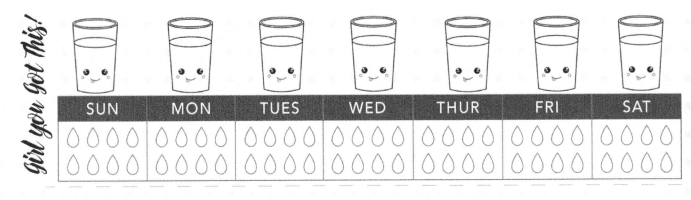

SUN	MON	TUES	WED	THUR	FRI	SAT

Girl you Got This!

3 Things I am Thankful For »

7 Goals For Next Week »»»»

Notes »

Getting Things Done For The Week of: _____

things to do

Habit Tracker

HABIT	S	M	T	W	T	F	S	REWARD

Water
(Check The Circle For 8 Glass Daily)

Girl you Got This!

SUN	MON	TUES	WED	THUR	FRI	SAT
○○○○	○○○○	○○○○	○○○○	○○○○	○○○○	○○○○
○○○○	○○○○	○○○○	○○○○	○○○○	○○○○	○○○○

3 Things I am Thankful For »

7 Goals For Next Week »»»»

Notes »

Getting Things Done For The Week of: _____

things to do

Habit Tracker

HABIT	S	M	T	W	T	F	S	REWARD

Water
(Check The Circle For 8 Glass Daily)

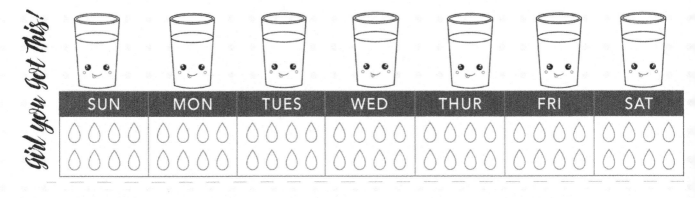

SUN	MON	TUES	WED	THUR	FRI	SAT
○○○○	○○○○	○○○○	○○○○	○○○○	○○○○	○○○○
○○○○	○○○○	○○○○	○○○○	○○○○	○○○○	○○○○

Girl you Got This!

3 Things I am Thankful For »

7 Goals For Next Week »»»»

Notes »

Getting Things Done For The Week of: _____

things to do

Habit Tracker

HABIT	S	M	T	W	T	F	S	REWARD

Water
(Check The Circle For 8 Glass Daily)

Girl you Got This!

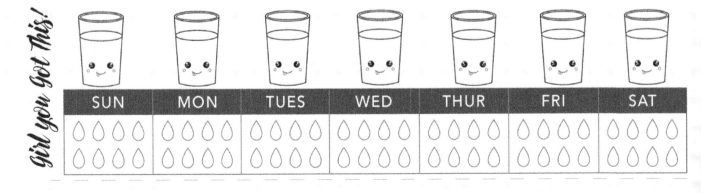

SUN	MON	TUES	WED	THUR	FRI	SAT

3 Things I am Thankful For »

7 Goals For Next Week »»»»

Notes »

Getting Things Done For The Week of: _____

things to do

Habit Tracker

HABIT	S	M	T	W	T	F	S	REWARD

Water
(Check The Circle For 8 Glass Daily)

SUN	MON	TUES	WED	THUR	FRI	SAT

Girl you Got This!

3 Things I am Thankful For »

7 Goals For Next Week »»»»

Notes »

Getting Things Done For The Week Of: _____

things to do

Habit Tracker

HABIT	S	M	T	W	T	F	S	REWARD

Water
(Check The Circle For 8 Glass Daily)

Girl you Got This!

SUN	MON	TUES	WED	THUR	FRI	SAT

3 Things I am Thankful For »

7 Goals For Next Week »»»»

Notes »

Getting Things Done For The Week of: _____

things to do

Habit Tracker

HABIT	S	M	T	W	T	F	S	REWARD

Water
(Check The Circle For 8 Glass Daily)

SUN	MON	TUES	WED	THUR	FRI	SAT
○○○○	○○○○	○○○○	○○○○	○○○○	○○○○	○○○○
○○○○	○○○○	○○○○	○○○○	○○○○	○○○○	○○○○

Girl you Got This!

3 Things I am Thankful For »

7 Goals For Next Week »»»»

Notes »

Getting Things Done For The Week of: _____

things to do

Habit Tracker

HABIT	S	M	T	W	T	F	S	REWARD

Water
(Check The Circle For 8 Glass Daily)

3 Things I am Thankful For »

7 Goals For Next Week »»»»

Notes »

Getting Things Done For The Week of: _____

things to do

Habit Tracker

HABIT	S	M	T	W	T	F	S	REWARD

Water
(Check The Circle For 8 Glass Daily)

Girl you Got This!

SUN	MON	TUES	WED	THUR	FRI	SAT

3 Things I am Thankful For »

7 Goals For Next Week »»»»

Notes »

Getting Things Done For The Week Of: _____

things to do

Habit Tracker

HABIT	S	M	T	W	T	F	S	REWARD

Water
(Check The Circle For 8 Glass Daily)

Girl you Got This!

SUN	MON	TUES	WED	THUR	FRI	SAT

3 Things I am Thankful For »

7 Goals For Next Week »»»»

Notes »

Getting Things Done For The Week of: _____

things to do

Habit Tracker

HABIT	S	M	T	W	T	F	S	REWARD

Water
(Check The Circle For 8 Glass Daily)

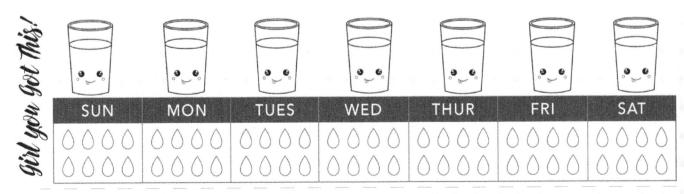

Girl you Got This!

3 Things I am Thankful For »

7 Goals For Next Week »»»»

Notes »

Getting Things Done For The Week of: _____

things to do

Habit Tracker

HABIT	S	M	T	W	T	F	S	REWARD

Water
(Check The Circle For 8 Glass Daily)

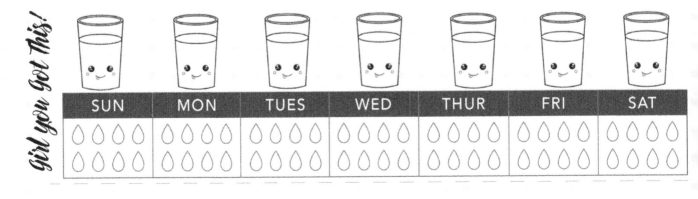

Girl you Got This!

SUN	MON	TUES	WED	THUR	FRI	SAT

3 Things I am Thankful For »

7 Goals For Next Week »»»»

Notes »

Getting Things Done For The Week of: _____

things to do

Habit Tracker

HABIT	S	M	T	W	T	F	S	REWARD

Water
(Check The Circle For 8 Glass Daily)

Girl you Got This!

SUN	MON	TUES	WED	THUR	FRI	SAT
○○○○	○○○○	○○○○	○○○○	○○○○	○○○○	○○○○
○○○○	○○○○	○○○○	○○○○	○○○○	○○○○	○○○○

3 Things I am Thankful For »

7 Goals For Next Week »»»»

Notes »

Getting Things Done For The Week of: _____

things to do

Habit Tracker

HABIT	S	M	T	W	T	F	S	REWARD

Water
(Check The Circle For 8 Glass Daily)

Girl you Got This!

SUN	MON	TUES	WED	THUR	FRI	SAT

3 Things I am Thankful For »

7 Goals For Next Week »»»»»

Notes »

Getting Things Done For The Week Of: _____

things to do

Habit Tracker

HABIT	S	M	T	W	T	F	S	REWARD

Water
(Check The Circle For 8 Glass Daily)

Girl you Got This!

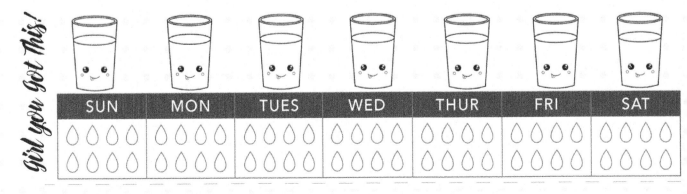

3 Things I am Thankful For »

7 Goals For Next Week »»»»

Notes »

Getting Things Done For The Week of: _____

things to do

Habit Tracker

HABIT	S	M	T	W	T	F	S	REWARD

Water
(Check The Circle For 8 Glass Daily)

Girl you Got This!

3 Things I am Thankful For »

7 Goals For Next Week »»»»

Notes »

Getting Things Done For The Week Of: _____

things to do

Habit Tracker

HABIT	S	M	T	W	T	F	S	REWARD

Water
(Check The Circle For 8 Glass Daily)

Girl you Got This!

3 Things I am Thankful For »

7 Goals For Next Week »»»»

Notes »

Getting Things Done For The Week Of: _____

things to do

Habit Tracker

HABIT	S	M	T	W	T	F	S	REWARD

Water
(Check The Circle For 8 Glass Daily)

Girl you Got This!

SUN	MON	TUES	WED	THUR	FRI	SAT

3 Things I am Thankful For »

7 Goals For Next Week »»»»

Notes »

Getting Things Done For The Week of: _____

things to do

Habit Tracker

HABIT	S	M	T	W	T	F	S	REWARD

Water
(Check The Circle For 8 Glass Daily)

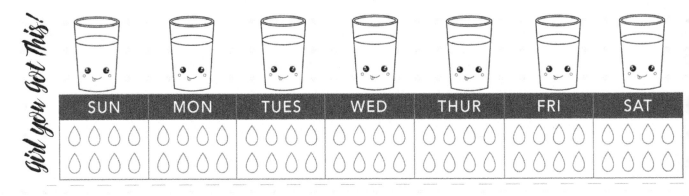

Girl you Got This!

SUN	MON	TUES	WED	THUR	FRI	SAT
○○○○	○○○○	○○○○	○○○○	○○○○	○○○○	○○○○
○○○○	○○○○	○○○○	○○○○	○○○○	○○○○	○○○○

3 Things I am Thankful For »

7 Goals For Next Week »»»»

Notes »

Getting Things Done For The Week Of: _____

things to do

Habit Tracker

HABIT	S	M	T	W	T	F	S	REWARD

Water
(Check The Circle For 8 Glass Daily)

Girl you Got This!

SUN	MON	TUES	WED	THUR	FRI	SAT

3 Things I am Thankful For »

7 Goals For Next Week »»»»

Notes »

Getting Things Done For The Week Of: _____

things to do

Habit Tracker

HABIT	S	M	T	W	T	F	S	REWARD

Water
(Check The Circle For 8 Glass Daily)

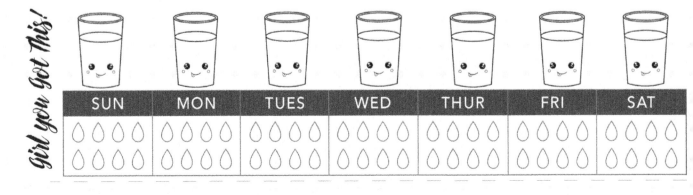

SUN	MON	TUES	WED	THUR	FRI	SAT

Girl you Got This!

3 Things I am Thankful For »

7 Goals For Next Week »»»»

Notes »

Getting Things Done For The Week Of: _____

things to do

Habit Tracker

HABIT	S	M	T	W	T	F	S	REWARD

Water
(Check The Circle For 8 Glass Daily)

Girl you Got This!

SUN	MON	TUES	WED	THUR	FRI	SAT

3 Things I am Thankful For »

7 Goals For Next Week »»»»»

Notes »

Getting Things Done For The Week of: _____

things to do

Habit Tracker

HABIT	S	M	T	W	T	F	S	REWARD

Water
(Check The Circle For 8 Glass Daily)

Girl you Got This!

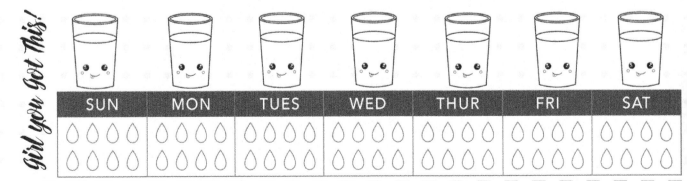

SUN	MON	TUES	WED	THUR	FRI	SAT

3 Things I am Thankful For »

7 Goals For Next Week »»»»

Notes »

Getting Things Done For The Week of: _____

things to do

Habit Tracker

HABIT	S	M	T	W	T	F	S	REWARD

Water
(Check The Circle For 8 Glass Daily)

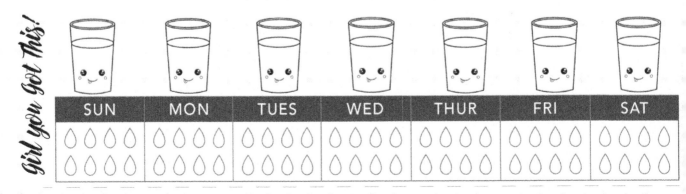

SUN	MON	TUES	WED	THUR	FRI	SAT

Girl you Got This!

3 Things I am Thankful For »

7 Goals For Next Week »»»»

Notes »

Getting Things Done For The Week of: _____

things to do

Habit Tracker

HABIT	S	M	T	W	T	F	S	REWARD

Water
(Check The Circle For 8 Glass Daily)

Girl you Got This!

3 Things I am Thankful For »

7 Goals For Next Week »»»»

Notes »

Getting Things Done For The Week of: _____

things to do

Habit Tracker

HABIT	S	M	T	W	T	F	S	REWARD

Water
(Check The Circle For 8 Glass Daily)

Girl you Got This!

SUN	MON	TUES	WED	THUR	FRI	SAT

3 Things I am Thankful For »

7 Goals For Next Week »»»»

Notes »

Getting Things Done For The Week of: _____

things to do

Habit Tracker

HABIT	S	M	T	W	T	F	S	REWARD

Water
(Check The Circle For 8 Glass Daily)

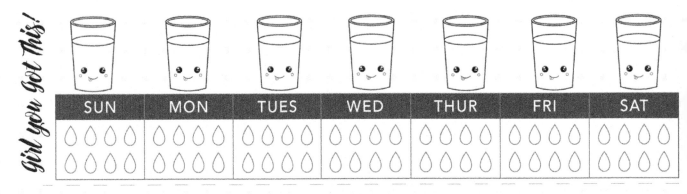

Girl you Got This!

SUN	MON	TUES	WED	THUR	FRI	SAT

3 Things I am Thankful For »

7 Goals For Next Week »»»»

Notes »

Getting Things Done For The Week Of: _____

things to do

Habit Tracker

HABIT	S	M	T	W	T	F	S	REWARD

Water
(Check The Circle For 8 Glass Daily)

3 Things I am Thankful For »

7 Goals For Next Week »»»»

Notes »

Getting Things Done For The Week of: _____

things to do

Habit Tracker

HABIT	S	M	T	W	T	F	S	REWARD

Water
(Check The Circle For 8 Glass Daily)

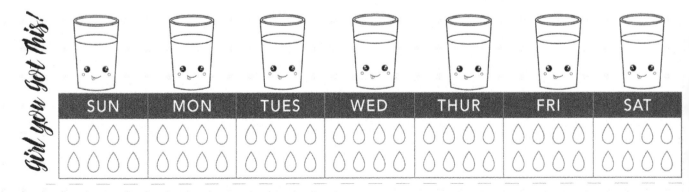

Girl you Got This!

SUN	MON	TUES	WED	THUR	FRI	SAT

3 Things I am Thankful For »

7 Goals For Next Week »»»»

Notes »

Getting Things Done For The Week Of: _____

things to do

Habit Tracker

HABIT	S	M	T	W	T	F	S	REWARD

Water
(Check The Circle For 8 Glass Daily)

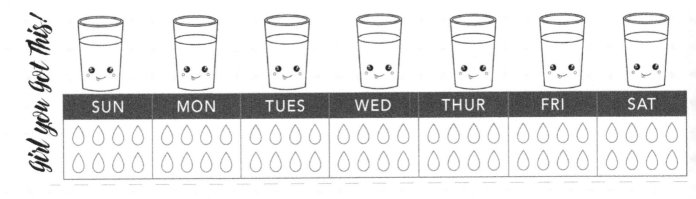

SUN	MON	TUES	WED	THUR	FRI	SAT

Girl you Got This!

3 Things I am Thankful For »

7 Goals For Next Week »»»»

Notes »

Getting Things Done For The Week of: _____

things to do

Habit Tracker

HABIT	S	M	T	W	T	F	S	REWARD

Water
(Check The Circle For 8 Glass Daily)

Girl you Got This!

SUN	MON	TUES	WED	THUR	FRI	SAT

3 Things I am Thankful For »

7 Goals For Next Week »»»»

Notes »

Getting Things Done For The Week of: _____

things to do

Habit Tracker

HABIT	S	M	T	W	T	F	S	REWARD

Water
(Check The Circle For 8 Glass Daily)

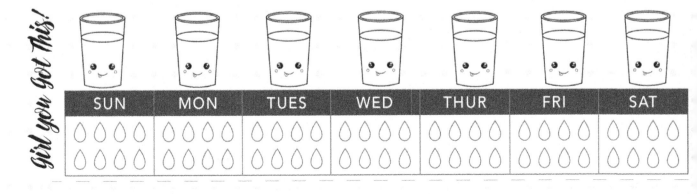

SUN	MON	TUES	WED	THUR	FRI	SAT

Girl you Got This!

3 Things I am Thankful For »

7 Goals For Next Week »»»»

Notes »

Getting Things Done For The Week of: _____

things to do

Habit Tracker

HABIT	S	M	T	W	T	F	S	REWARD

Water
(Check The Circle For 8 Glass Daily)

Girl you Got This!

3 Things I am Thankful For »

7 Goals For Next Week »»»»

Notes »

Getting Things Done For The Week of: _____

things to do

Habit Tracker

HABIT	S	M	T	W	T	F	S	REWARD

Water
(Check The Circle For 8 Glass Daily)

Girl you Got This!

SUN	MON	TUES	WED	THUR	FRI	SAT

3 Things I am Thankful For »

7 Goals For Next Week »»»»

Notes »

Getting Things Done For The Week of: _____

things to do

Habit Tracker

HABIT	S	M	T	W	T	F	S	REWARD

Water
(Check The Circle For 8 Glass Daily)

Girl you Got This!

SUN	MON	TUES	WED	THUR	FRI	SAT

3 Things I am Thankful For »

7 Goals For Next Week »»»»

Notes »

Getting Things Done For The Week Of: _____

things to do

Habit Tracker

HABIT	S	M	T	W	T	F	S	REWARD

Water
(Check The Circle For 8 Glass Daily)

Girl you Got This!

SUN	MON	TUES	WED	THUR	FRI	SAT

3 Things I am Thankful For »

7 Goals For Next Week »»»»

Notes »

Getting Things Done For The Week of: _____

things to do

Habit Tracker

HABIT	S	M	T	W	T	F	S	REWARD

Water
(Check The Circle For 8 Glass Daily)

Girl you Got This!

SUN	MON	TUES	WED	THUR	FRI	SAT

3 Things I am Thankful For »

7 Goals For Next Week »»»»

Notes »

Getting Things Done For The Week Of: _____

things to do

Habit Tracker

HABIT	S	M	T	W	T	F	S	REWARD

Water
(Check The Circle For 8 Glass Daily)

Girl you Got This!

SUN	MON	TUES	WED	THUR	FRI	SAT

3 Things I am Thankful For »

7 Goals For Next Week »»»»

Notes »

Getting Things Done For The Week of: _____

things to do

Habit Tracker

HABIT	S	M	T	W	T	F	S	REWARD

Water
(Check The Circle For 8 Glass Daily)

Girl you Got This!

SUN	MON	TUES	WED	THUR	FRI	SAT

3 Things I am Thankful For »

7 Goals For Next Week »»»»

Notes »

Getting Things Done For The Week Of: _____

things to do

Habit Tracker

HABIT	S	M	T	W	T	F	S	REWARD

Water
(Check The Circle For 8 Glass Daily)

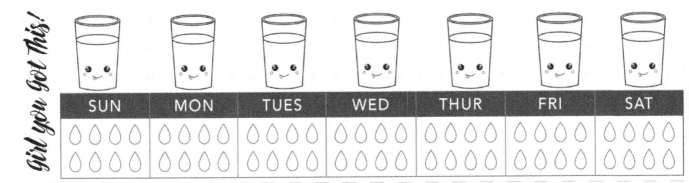

Girl you Got This!

SUN	MON	TUES	WED	THUR	FRI	SAT

3 Things I am Thankful For »

7 Goals For Next Week »»»»

Notes »

Getting Things Done For The Week of: _____

things to do

Habit Tracker

HABIT	S	M	T	W	T	F	S	REWARD

Water
(Check The Circle For 8 Glass Daily)

SUN	MON	TUES	WED	THUR	FRI	SAT

Girl you Got This!

3 Things I am Thankful For »

7 Goals For Next Week »»»»

Notes »

Getting Things Done For The Week Of: _____

things to do

Habit Tracker

HABIT	S	M	T	W	T	F	S	REWARD

Water
(Check The Circle For 8 Glass Daily)

SUN	MON	TUES	WED	THUR	FRI	SAT

Girl you Got This!

3 Things I am Thankful For »

7 Goals For Next Week »»»»

Notes »

Getting Things Done For The Week of: _____

things to do

Habit Tracker

HABIT	S	M	T	W	T	F	S	REWARD

Water
(Check The Circle For 8 Glass Daily)

Girl you Got This!

3 Things I am Thankful For »

7 Goals For Next Week »»»»

Notes »

Getting Things Done For The Week of: _____

things to do

Habit Tracker

HABIT	S	M	T	W	T	F	S	REWARD

Water
(Check The Circle For 8 Glass Daily)

Girl you Got This!

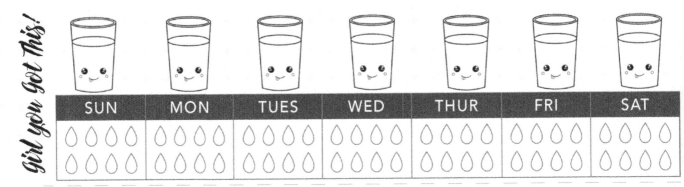

SUN	MON	TUES	WED	THUR	FRI	SAT

3 Things I am Thankful For »

7 Goals For Next Week »»»»

Notes »

Getting Things Done For The Week of: _____

things to do

Habit Tracker

HABIT	S	M	T	W	T	F	S	REWARD

Water
(Check The Circle For 8 Glass Daily)

SUN	MON	TUES	WED	THUR	FRI	SAT

Girl you Got This!

3 Things I am Thankful For »

7 Goals For Next Week »»»»

Notes »

Getting Things Done For The Week Of: _____

things to do

Habit Tracker

HABIT	S	M	T	W	T	F	S	REWARD

Water
(Check The Circle For 8 Glass Daily)

Girl you Got This!

SUN	MON	TUES	WED	THUR	FRI	SAT

3 Things I am Thankful For »

7 Goals For Next Week »»»»

Notes »

Getting Things Done For The Week of: _____

things to do

Habit Tracker

HABIT	S	M	T	W	T	F	S	REWARD

Water
(Check The Circle For 8 Glass Daily)

3 Things I am Thankful For »

7 Goals For Next Week »»»»

Notes »

Getting Things Done For The Week Of: _____

things to do

Habit Tracker

HABIT	S	M	T	W	T	F	S	REWARD

Water
(Check The Circle For 8 Glass Daily)

Girl you Got This!

SUN	MON	TUES	WED	THUR	FRI	SAT

3 Things I am Thankful For »

7 Goals For Next Week »»»»

Notes »

Getting Things Done For The Week of: _____

things to do

Habit Tracker

HABIT	S	M	T	W	T	F	S	REWARD

Water
(Check The Circle For 8 Glass Daily)

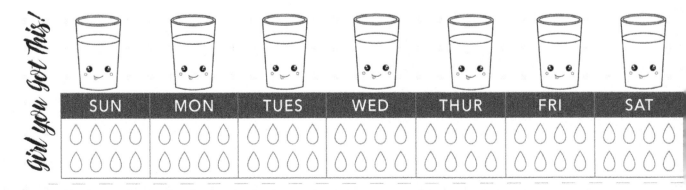

Girl you Got This!

SUN	MON	TUES	WED	THUR	FRI	SAT

3 Things I am Thankful For »

7 Goals For Next Week »»»»

Notes »

Getting Things Done For The Week Of: _____

things to do

Habit Tracker

HABIT	S	M	T	W	T	F	S	REWARD

Water
(Check The Circle For 8 Glass Daily)

Girl you Got This!

SUN	MON	TUES	WED	THUR	FRI	SAT

3 Things I am Thankful For »

7 Goals For Next Week »»»»

Notes »

Getting Things Done For The Week of: _____

things to do

Habit Tracker

HABIT	S	M	T	W	T	F	S	REWARD

Water
(Check The Circle For 8 Glass Daily)

Girl you Got This!

SUN	MON	TUES	WED	THUR	FRI	SAT
⬡⬡⬡⬡	⬡⬡⬡⬡	⬡⬡⬡⬡	⬡⬡⬡⬡	⬡⬡⬡⬡	⬡⬡⬡⬡	⬡⬡⬡⬡
⬡⬡⬡⬡	⬡⬡⬡⬡	⬡⬡⬡⬡	⬡⬡⬡⬡	⬡⬡⬡⬡	⬡⬡⬡⬡	⬡⬡⬡⬡

3 Things I am Thankful For »

7 Goals For Next Week »»»»

Notes »

Getting Things Done For The Week Of: _____

things to do

Habit Tracker

HABIT	S	M	T	W	T	F	S	REWARD

Water
(Check The Circle For 8 Glass Daily)

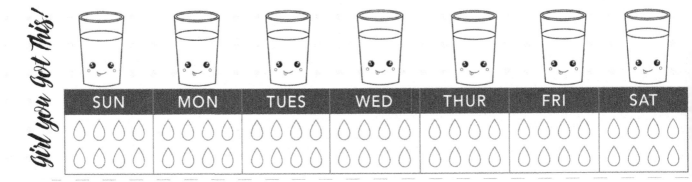

SUN	MON	TUES	WED	THUR	FRI	SAT

3 Things I am Thankful For »

7 Goals For Next Week »»»»

Notes »

Thanks

We acknowledge the two drifters for the Bucket list Ideas used in this Journal.

Also we appreciate you for believing in Us and Buying this Journal. May all Your Dreams Come through this Year!

Visit: **Cobis Cute Press** on **amazon.com** for more of this Journal to Create A Planner For The Year.

Made in the USA
Monee, IL
11 June 2020